# HAD



*(peace be upon him)*

Rashid Ahmad Chaudhry

Islam International Publications Limited

Hadhrat Nuh *(peace be upon him)*

Author: Rashid Ahmad Chaudhry

First published in UK in 2005



Published by:
Islam International Publications Limited
"Islamabad"
Sheephatch Lane
Tilford,Surrey GU10 2AQ
UK

Printed at:
Raqeem Press,Tilford,U.K



ISBN: 1 85372 758 X

CONTENTS

# IMPORTANT NOTES

1. All references in this book are from the Holy Qur'an except where particularly specified.

2. *Bismillah-ir-Rahman-ir Raheem* is considered to be the first verse of the chapter if the chapter of the Holy Qur'an begins with it.

3. The Muslim readers are requested to say "peace be upon him" whenever the name of a Prophet appears in the text.

4. We have included only those events in the story of Hadhrat Nuh from the Bible, which are not inconsistent with the Holy Qur'an because the Holy Qur'an has remained unchanged since it was revealed. Allah safeguards the text of the Holy Qur'an while there have been interpolations and changes made in the Bible from time to time.

Children's Book Committee

# INTRODUCTION

The book 'Hadhrat Nuh' deals with the life history of an ancient Prophet Hadhrat Nuh, peace be upon him, a Law bearing Prophet sent by God Almighty.
It is related that during his time people had started worshipping idols. They had fallen into the depth of moral and spiritual darkness. Hadhrat Nuh tried to bring them back to Allah but only a few came to his fold while most of them rejected the message of Allah and treated Hadhrat Nuh with contempt. They even threatened him with stoning and expulsion from the town.
Hadhrat Nuh prayed to God Almighty to make judgment between him and his people who rejected him. Allah decided to punish the wrongdoers and save the believers. A mighty flood came and the non-believers were drowned while the believers were all saved in the ark.

Allah says in the Holy Qur'an:
"Indeed in the stories of the Prophets there is a lesson for men of understanding." (12:112)

The Children's Book Committee was established by Hadhrat Khalifatul-Masih IV and had been working under his guidance. After his demise in April 2003 the Committee continued its work under the guidance and supervision of Hadhrat Khalkifatul-Masih V. We thank the chairman of the Book Committee, Rashid Ahmad Chaudhry and his team namely Mansoor Saqi, Masroor Ahmad and Syed Muhammad Arif Nasser for the publication of this book. May Allah bless them for their dedication and hard work and reward them abundantly in this world and the Hereafter.
The readers may like to test their knowledge by answering questions, which are given at the end.
A glossary of difficult words is also provided.

Munir-ud-Din Shams,
Additional Vakil-ut-Tasneef, London.

# HADHRAT ADAM TO HADHRAT NUH

(According to the Bible)

ADAM

SETH

ENOSH

KENAN

MAHALALEL

JARED

ENOCH (IDREES)

METHUSELAH

LAMECH

NOAH (NUH)

# HADHRAT NUH

*(peace be upon him)*

## HISTORICAL BACKGROUND

In ancient times, there lived a Prophet called Hadhrat Nuh or Noah, peace be upon him. The Bible tells us that his father's name was Lamech and that he lived nine generations after Hadhrat Adam, peace be upon him.

Hadhrat Nuh was a Law-bearing Prophet meaning that he brought Shariah, a Divine Law. The Law was revealed to him because in his time the human mind had reached such a stage of development that it was able to understand and comprehend Divine attributes. Moreover, as people in Hadhrat Nuh's time laid down the foundation of human civilization, those evils that normally appear in a civilized society began to appear in them. So a Divine Law was needed to guide mankind to the right path.

There are two kinds of Prophets sent by God Almighty. Some Prophets bring a new Law or Shariah. There are others who do not bring a new Law but follow the Law or Shariah of the previous Law- Bearing Prophet.

The Bible tells us that Noah was a righteous man, blameless among the people of his time, and he walked with God.[1] 'Walking with God,' means that all his acts were according to the Will of God. He lived in a valley surrounded by huge mountains in Mesopotamia in Southern Iraq. There were a great many springs flowing from the mountains in that area.

# THE AGE OF HADHRAT NUH

The Holy Qur'an says, "Certainly We sent Nuh to his people and he lived among them a thousand years less fifty."[2]
Therefore his age is mentioned as 950 years in the Holy Qur'an while the Bible gives his age as 952 years. This does not mean that he lived for 950 or 952 years. It is difficult to determine his actual age. Only Allah knows best. The period, which the Holy Qur'an or the Bible describes, is not the span of Hadhrat Nuh's physical life. This period is in fact the time Hadhrat Nuh's teachings lasted. The Shariah introduced through him remained in force for about one thousand years. Many Prophets followed this law until God revealed a new one. It extended to the time of Hadhrat Ibrahim, peace be upon him, as he followed Hadhrat Nuh's Shariah. It seems that the first fifty years of Hadhrat Nuh's ministry were the years of spiritual progress for his community after which the spiritual condition of his followers began to deteriorate. This deterioration became complete in nine hundred years.

# PEOPLE RETURN TO IDOL WORSHIP

The people of Hadhrat Nuh's time had become corrupt. Instead of worshipping the One and Only God they had started to worship idols made of wood or stone. They had many idols. Five of them were very popular. Their names were Wadd, Suwa, Yaghuth, Yauq and Nasr. It is said that people at the time of Hadhrat Nuh used to make statues in memory of their pious people who were long dead and place them where these pious people used to sit. Later they deviated from the true path and started worshipping them. They were convinced that the idols would help them in their time of need so they used to beg everything from the idols. They followed the beliefs of their forefathers who were idol worshippers.

WADD was an idol made in the shape of a man. This god represented manly power.

SUWA was in the shape of a woman. This god represented female beauty.

YAGHUTH: They believed that this god would rescue them from hardship.

YAUQ was in the shape of a horse representing speed. They believed that this particular god would come quickly in order to prevent their enemy from doing harm to them.

NASR was in the shape of an eagle representing long life.

God Almighty sent Hadhrat Nuh, peace be upon him, to bring the people back to the worship of One God. He told Hadhrat Nuh, peace be upon him, to invite his people to the way of Allah with love and wisdom.

## HADHRAT NUH CONVEYS THE MESSAGE OF THE UNITY OF GOD

Hadhrat Nuh was sent to his people with a divine revealed Law. He called his people to God, to the path of success and salvation. He emphasized to them the unity of God. He said to them, "O, my people, worship Allah alone, you have no God other than Him. Will you not then fear God and become righteous?"[3]

The message was delivered to them politely and with wisdom but they were not prepared to listen to him, rather they ignored him and ran away from him.

Hadhrat Nuh, peace be upon him, was very sad by such treatment at the hands of his people. Addressing his Lord he said, "My Lord, I have called my people day and night, but my calling them has only made them flee from me all the more. Whenever I called them in the hope that You might forgive them, they put their fingers into their ears and wrapped their garments around them and persisted in their wickedness and behaved with extreme arrogance. Then I invited them to your path openly. I preached to them in public and also spoke to them in private. I told them to seek forgiveness of their Lord, for He is Most Forgiving. He will send down rain for you in abundance, and He will strengthen you with wealth and with children and will bestow gardens on you and will cause rivers to flow for you."[4]

The chiefs rejected Hadhrat Nuh by saying: "Surely we see you to be in manifest error."[5]

He said, "O, my people there is no error in me. I am a Messenger from the Lord of the Worlds. I deliver to you the messages from your Lord and give you sincere advice and I know from Allah what you do not know." [6]

He told them that he could not be in error, for he had come from God, therefore there was no possibility for him to move away from the path that leads to God.

He advised them to accept the message from Allah and become righteous. He warned them of the evil consequences of the rejection of the divine message, but all his preaching and warnings fell on deaf ears. They accused him of falsehood and ridiculed him. Instead of following him they followed their own leaders, who incited them to oppose Hadhrat Nuh.

Despite the bitter opposition of the chiefs, Hadhrat Nuh continued preaching. He was firm in his resolve and knew very well that he was doing everything to please his Lord. He tried everything to convince his people of the truth of his message. He repeatedly asked them not to revolt against the Most Merciful God, Who had created them and provided them with food and shelter.

Once, there was no rain for a long time. The crops withered and the fruit gardens dried up. Hadhrat Nuh, peace be upon him, told his people that God was displeased with them because of their misdeeds. He told them that if they became true believers, God would send down rain for them in abundance and would grant them an increase in wealth and bless them with children. He will also cause their gardens to grow and rivers to flow for them and they would prosper as a result. Hadhrat Nuh's people, however, rejected him outright.

The leaders of the disbelievers told their people, "He is only a man like yourselves, yet he seeks to make himself superior to you. If Allah has so willed, He could surely have sent down angels. We have never heard of such a thing among our forefathers. He is only a man stricken with madness; wait, therefore, concerning him for a while."[7]

In ancient times many people found it difficult to believe that a Prophet could be an ordinary human being in appearance. They thought that he should have many heads or hands. So the enemies of Hadhrat Nuh raised an objection against him saying that if he was really a true Prophet, his appearance should have been different from theirs.
They also accused him of trying to impose his authority on them. They told him that they would not listen to him as his teachings were opposed to the beliefs of their forefathers. They

branded him a liar and accused him of madness and hoped that he would soon perish.
Hadhrat Nuh, peace be upon him, said to his people, “Fear Allah and obey me. I do not ask of you any reward for this, for my reward rests only with the Lord of the worlds.”[8]
He said, “I do not say to you that I possess the treasures of Allah or that I know the unseen or that I am an angel.”[9]
He said, “O my people! Surely I am a plain Warner unto you.”[10]

The arguments between Hadhrat Nuh, peace be upon him, and his people continued for a long time.
The chiefs of his people used to laugh at him saying that none of the prominent people had accepted him therefore he was bound to fail. They asked Hadhrat Nuh to drive away those who had become his followers, as they were the people who had no status in the society and whose faith was insincere.
They said: “How can we believe you when we see that only the mean and lowly people have become your followers?”[11]
Hadhrat Nuh, peace be upon him, replied that he had no knowledge of what his followers had been doing in the past. Their past actions were God’s concern alone. All that matters is that they were the believers and had submitted to the Will of Allah. He told them that his task was to keep them on the right path and away from evil. It was therefore not proper for him to drive his followers away simply because they happened to be of humble origin. Such an act would certainly incur God’s displeasure. He told them that they might call the believers insincere, weak in faith, mean and lowly but after obeying the commands of Allah they had become the blessed people and respectable in the sight of Allah while those who are non-believers, were indeed ignorant.

The people did not like Hadhrat Nuh preaching to them. They told him that if he did not stop preaching to them, they would stone him.
Hadhrat Nuh warned them of God's punishment. He told them to stop worshipping idols. He said, "O, my people, worship Allah. You have no other God but Him. Indeed I fear for you the punishment of the great day".[12]
They replied: "Certainly you disputed with us long and indeed many a time. So bring now that with which you have threatened us, if you are speaking the truth."[13]
Hadhrat Nuh, peace be upon him, replied, "Allah alone will bring it to you if He Wills and you will not be able to frustrate God's purpose. If Allah intends to destroy you, my admonishment will not profit you, however much I desire to admonish you. He is your Lord and to Him shall you be made to return."[14]

Sometimes he would say to them, "What is the matter with you that you do not give dignity to Allah? Certainly He has created you in stages. Have you not observed how Allah has created seven heavens tier upon tier, and has placed the moon therein as a light and made the sun as a lamp?
Remember that Allah has created you from the earth like the raising of vegetation. Then He will return you therein and bring you forth in a special way, when you will get a new life in the Hereafter. God has made the earth for you an enormous place so that you may travel on its open routes and wide paths."[15]
Even such arguments had no effect on them and they continued to ignore the Signs of Allah.
Hadhrat Nuh employed all means to make his people listen to the divine message, but all his efforts became fruitless. The chiefs of his people devised a mighty plan against him. They said to one another that they should get together and oppose him with all their might. They told their people "Do not

forsake your gods under any circumstances. Do not forsake Wadd, Suwa, Yaghuth, Yauq or Nasr."[16]

They carried on worshipping idols and treated Hadhrat Nuh in utter contempt. Only a handful of people believed in him. Even his wife and son were among the non-believers. Naturally Hadhrat Nuh was very disappointed.

Hadhrat Nuh had great faith in the truth of his mission. He must have received assurances from God Almighty that he would succeed against his enemies. He therefore challenged his opponents and told them to use all their power and resources against him. He said to them, "O my people! If the position, which Allah has assigned to me, and my constantly reminding you of your duty through the Signs of Allah, offend you, then remember that my whole trust is in Allah. You should therefore decide upon a course of action after mutual consultation and get together your associates and leave no part of your course of action obscure. Then carry out your design against me and give me no respite."[17]

He warned them that even if they tried their utmost to put an end to his mission, they would not succeed because they were fighting against God.

As the opposition against Hadhrat Nuh, peace be upon him, increased tremendously, God revealed to him: "None of your people will believe except those who have already believed. Grieve not therefore at what they have been doing."[18]

After receiving this information from God Almighty that no more people would enter his fold, Hadhrat Nuh offered the following prayers to God Almighty:

"My Lord leave not in the land a single one of the disbelievers as dwellers therein; for if You leave them, they will only lead astray Your servants and will not give birth but to a sinner and a disbeliever."[19]

Allah decided to eliminate the disbelievers from the face of the earth. He commanded Hadhrat Nuh to build an ark, big enough, to accommodate all the believers.

## HADHRAT NUH BUILDS AN ARK

Allah said to Hadhrat Nuh:
"Build an ark under our eyes and as commanded by Our revelation and address not Me concerning the wrongdoers. They are surely going to be drowned." [20]
Hadhrat Nuh obeyed immediately and started building an ark of wood with the help of his followers. They brought wooden planks and nails. It was not an easy task. People were surprised. They could not see the reason for building such a huge ark. Every time the chiefs of his people passed by him, they laughed at him and thought that he had gone mad.
"Why are you making this ark? Will it float on land?" they would say. Hadhrat Nuh did not pay any heed to their mockery. He told them that their mockery could do him no harm, nor could it bring him into disgrace. It is they who would be humiliated as they were about to be overtaken by a punishment, which would not end in this life but would continue into the life to come.
Hadhrat Nuh, peace be upon him, prayed to God Almighty:
"My Lord! My people have treated me as a liar, so make judgment decisively between them and me and rescue me as well as the believers that are with me."[21]
On another occasion he prayed:
"I am overcome. O Allah! Come to my help."[22]
Allah heard his prayers and he along with his family members who believed in him, and his followers were eventually saved while the disbelievers were punished severely.

## THE MIGHTY FLOOD, A PUNISHMENT

Hadhrat Nuh lived in the part of the country where springs and fountains were in abundance. When Allah's command came, dark clouds appeared in the sky suddenly and rain began to fall in torrents. Water began to gush forth from the depth of the earth and springs and fountains began to sprout as well. There was water everywhere.

The Holy Quran says:

"We opened the gates of heaven, with water pouring down; and We caused the earth to burst forth with springs, so the two waters met for a purpose that was decreed."[23]

Some people believe that the flood came throughout the world. This is not true. It was not a universal phenomenon. It overtook only the people to whom Hadhrat Nuh was sent.

## THE ARK FLOATS WITH HADHRAT NUH, PEACE BE UPON HIM, AND HIS FOLLOWERS ON BOARD

Allah told Hadhrat Nuh, peace be upon him, to load the ark with all such animals that would be needed, a pair of each, male and female and bring his family on board, except those against whom God's judgment had already been passed. He also instructed him to bring on board all those who had accepted him as a Messenger of Allah. Hadhrat Nuh, peace be upon him, called his family members, who believed in him and all his followers and told them, "Embark therein. In the name of Allah, be its course and its mooring. Indeed my Lord is All Forgiving, Ever Merciful."[24]

Thus Allah told Hadhrat Nuh that the ark would float and finish its journey.

God Almighty taught Hadhrat Nuh some prayers. Hadhrat Nuh told his followers to recite those prayers after they had settled down in the ark. He told them to say, "All praise belongs to Allah, Who has saved us from the unjust people."[25]
He also told them to say "My Lord! Cause me to land a blessed landing, for You are the best of those who bring people to land."[26]

## ALLAH SAVES THE BELIEVERS

As the water rose and the flood increased rapidly on all sides, it covered the entire habitation. Everything on earth was under water while the ark floated safely on top.
Allah says, "We carried him upon that which was made of planks and nails. It floated on under Our eyes: a reward for him who had been rejected and We left it as a Sign for the coming generations."[27]

Hadhrat Nuh saw his son who had joined the disbelievers. According to some his name was Yam. Hadhrat Nuh saw him drifting away in swirling waters. He called out to him, "My son, climb on the ark with us and be not among the disbelievers."[28]
He replied, "I shall soon climb on a mountain, which will shelter me from the water."[29]
Hadhrat Nuh replied, "There is no shelter for anyone this day from the decree of Allah, except those to whom He shows mercy."[30]
Suddenly a wave came between them and took his son away. Hadhrat Nuh was naturally sad to see his son drown before his eyes. He cried to God Almighty, "O my Lord, my son is of my family. Surely Your promise is true and You are the Most Just of the judges."[31]

Hadhrat Nuh thought that God had promised to save all members of his family. In fact when Allah promised to save the members of his family, He meant only those members of his family who were believers and had established a true relationship with God through him.

In response to Hadhrat Nuh's request Allah said, "O, Nuh, your son is surely not of your family. He is indeed a man of unrighteous conduct. So do not ask Me about that of which you have no knowledge. I admonish you lest you should become one of the ignorant people."[32]

Hadhrat Nuh said, "My Lord! I seek refuge in you lest I should ask of you anything of which I have no knowledge, so unless You forgive me and have mercy upon me, I shall be one of the losers."[33]

Thus Hadhrat Nuh, peace be upon him, realised that he had not fully understood Allah's promise. He sought Allah's forgiveness. It became clear to him that everyone is accountable for his actions and that a Prophet's son is no exception.

As regards his wife, she was described as an evil person who was bent upon rejecting the truth. So the companionship, even of a Prophet of God, did not save her from Allah's punishment. The Holy Quran says: "Allah gives as examples of disbelievers the wife of Nuh and the wife of Lot. They were married to two righteous servants of Ours, but they acted disloyally towards them. So their husbands availed them naught against Allah and they were told; enter the Fire along with those who enter therein."[34]

## THE ARK RESTS ON A MOUNTAIN

It was a mighty flood. The ark floated on waves as high as mountains. Even the tops of the mountains were under water.

God rescued Hadhrat Nuh and those with him in the ark, while those who rejected him were drowned as a punishment.

Then God caused rain to stop and the floodwater was made to subside and the ark came to rest on a mountain called Al Judi.[35] According to the Bible, "The ark came to rest on the mountains of Ararat."[36]

Many people including historians, geographers and research scholars have tried to locate these mountains, but their research varied and they could not determine precisely in which country these mountains were situated. Various countries including Turkey, Armenia and Iran claim that both mountains, Al-Judi and Ararat lie in their domains.

According to the Bible, when the ark stopped, Hadhrat Nuh released a raven to find out whether there was any dry land around where the ark stopped. The raven could not find any place to set its feet because there was water everywhere; so it returned to Hadhrat Nuh in the ark. After several attempts Hadhrat Nuh sent out a dove. When the dove returned to him in the evening, in its beak was a freshly plucked olive leaf. Then Hadhrat Nuh was convinced that water had receded completely from the ground and that they would be able to disembark safely.

## GLAD TIDINGS TO HADHRAT NUH AND HIS FOLLOWERS

The olive leaf was also a sign that Allah had blessed Hadhrat Nuh, his people and their future generations. They would be strong in their faith and perfect in their sacrifices. Allah says in the Holy Quran:

"We saved him and those who were with him in the ark. And We made them inheritors of the land, while We drowned those who rejected Our Signs. See then, how was the end of those who had been warned."[37]

At another place in the Holy Quran God says:
"Nuh indeed did cry unto us, and what an excellent answer did We give to his prayer!
We saved him and his family from the great distress; and We made his offspring the only survivors and We left for him a good name among the following generations. Peace be upon Nuh among the people of the worlds. Thus indeed We reward those who do good. He was surely one of Our believing servants.[38]
Hadhrat Nuh, peace be upon him, told his people that God had conferred innumerable blessings on them and they could achieve greatness, a place of dignity and respect among the nations of the world by following the teachings which he had brought.
It so happened that in this new land Allah bestowed prosperity to Hadhrat Nuh and his followers. They laid the foundation of human civilization and culture and as their culture became strong their numbers also began to increase. On the other hand the number of less civilized communities living with them in the same land or in the surrounding lands began to decrease. The descendants of Hadhrat Nuh being more civilized and having more material resources at their disposal seemed to have spread to other lands and in the course of time absorbed some of the less civilised people.
Three sons of Hadhrat Nuh, peace be upon him, namely Shem, Ham and Japeth are generally believed to be the ancestors of the three principal races of mankind.

Another great blessing bestowed upon Ḣadhrat Nuh' descendents was that Allah promised to continue Prophethood in his progeny.

Allah says:

"We sent Nuh and Ibrahim, and We bestowed Prophethood and the Book upon their descendants. Some of them followed the guidance but many of them were rebellious."[39]

All praise belongs to Allah, Lord of the worlds.

## QUESTIONS

1. How many generations after Hadhrat Adam did Hadhrat Nuh appear, according to the Bible?
2. Did Hadhrat Nuh bring a new divine Law?
3. The Bible says, "Noah walked with God." What does this mean?
4. What is the name of the native country of Hadhrat Nuh?
5. What name was mentioned in the Bible for Hadhrat Nuh's father?
6. Some people believe that Hadhrat Nuh lived for 950 years. What is your opinion?
7. Name the five popular idols people worshipped during the time of Hadhrat Nuh.
8. What objections did the chiefs of people raise against Hadhrat Nuh?
9. Why did people mock Hadhrat Nuh when they saw him making an ark?
10. How many animals was Hadhrat Nuh allowed to take into the ark?
11. What do you know about the character of Hadhrat Nuh's son, who was not among his followers?
12. What was the reply of Hadhrat Nuh's son when Hadhrat Nuh asked him to join him in the ark?
13. What happened to him when the flood came?
14. Why did Hadhrat Nuh plead to Allah for the safety of his son?
15. What did Allah say in reply to his plea?
16. What punishment was given to the non-believers?
17. How were the family members, who believed in him and other followers of Hadhrat Nuh saved?

18. On which mountain did the ark rest according to the Qur'an?
19. On which mountain did the ark rest according to the Bible?
20. Where are these mountains situated?
21. What do you know of Hadhrat Nuh's wife?
22. Some people believe that the flood was universal. What is your opinion?
23. What method, according to the Bible, did Hadhrat Nuh employ to find out if the water had subsided?
24. What is the greatest blessing Allah has bestowed on the descendents of Hadhrat Nuh and Hadhrat Ibrahim?

# GLOSSARY

## A

| | |
|---|---|
| Ark | the wooden vessel, Hadhrat Nuh made |
| Arrogance | haughty |
| Astray | away from the right path |

## B

| | |
|---|---|
| Bounties | rewards |

## C

| | |
|---|---|
| Consequences | the results or effects of an action |

## D

| | |
|---|---|
| Deterioration | decline |
| Deviated | turned away |
| Disembark | get off from the ark |
| Displeasure | anger |
| Dwellers | residents, people who live there |
| Domains | the land controlled by a country |

## E

| | |
|---|---|
| Eliminate | to expel, to get rid of |
| Enormous | very large |
| Extinct | no longer in existence |

## F

| | |
|---|---|
| Fold | Jamaat |
| Forsake | give up, renounce |
| Frustrate | prevent |

## H

| | |
|---|---|
| Habitation | residences, homes |
| Handful | small number |
| Hereafter | the next world |
| Humiliated | humbled |

## I

| | |
|---|---|
| Innumerable | countless, many |
| Insincere | not loyal |
| Inheritor | someone who receives property after the death of a person |

## M

| | |
|---|---|
| Manifest | clear |
| Mockery | derision, ridicule, laugh at |

## O

| | |
|---|---|
| Obscure | hidden |

## P

| | |
|---|---|
| Prosper | succeed |
| Perish | suffer death |
| Progeny | descendants of a person |

## R

| | |
|---|---|
| Respite | temporary relief or break |
| Receded | went back, faded |

## S

| | |
|---|---|
| Shariah | Divine or religious law |
| Sprout | grow |

## T

| | |
|---|---|
| Tier | layer |

## U

| | |
|---|---|
| Unrighteous | sinful, wicked |

# REFERENCES


1 The Bible, Genesis (6:9)
2 Ch 29:15
3 Ch 23:24
4 Ch 71:6-13
5 Ch 7:61
6 Ch 7:62,63
7 Ch 23:25,26
8 Ch 26:109,110
9 Ch11:32
10 Ch 71:3
11 Ch 26:112
12 Ch 7:60
13 Ch11:33
14 Ch 11:34,35
15 Ch 71:14-21
16 Ch 71:24
17 Ch 10:72
18 Ch 11:37
19 Ch 71:27,28
20 Ch 11:38
21 Ch 26:118,119
22 Ch 54:11
23 Ch 54:12,13
24 Ch 11:42
25 Ch 23:29
26 Ch 23:30
27 Ch 54:14-16
28 Ch 11:43
29 Ch 11:44
30 Ch11:44
31 Ch 11:46
32 Ch 11:47
33 Ch 11:48
34 Ch 66:11
35 Ch 11:45
36 The Bible Genesis (8:4)
37 Ch 10:74
38 Ch 37: 76-82
39 Ch 57:27